BRAVURA COOL

BRAVURA COOL

JANE LEWTY

1913 Press
www.1913press.org
1913press@gmail.com

1913 is a not-for-profit collective. Contributions to 1913 Press may be tax-deductible.

Manufactured in the oldest country in the world, The United States of America.

Many thanks to all the artists, from this century and the last, who made this project possible.

This publication is supported in generous part by individual donors, named & unnamed:
Anonymous (x13), Robert J. Bertholf, Richard Dillard, Ectopistes Migratorius, Coco Owen,
Christopher Nealon, Kathleen Ossip, Marjorie Perloff, Jean-Jacques Poucel, Matvei Yankelevich.

1913 profusely thanks Le Board:
Eleanor Antin, Rae Armantrout, Thalia Field, Scarlett Higgins, Jen Hofer, Matthew Hofer,
Fanny Howe, Joseph Jeon, John Keene, Sawako Nakayasu, Claudia Rankine,
Jerome Rothenberg, Cole Swensen, John Yau.

Founder & Editrice: Sandra Doller
Vice-Editor & Designer: Ben Doller

Cover art: *Skigraph 1* (1999) by Sandra Lewty

ISBN: 9780984029747

CONTENTS:

The Better Condensed

Two weeks, languor-scored, I'm thinking of strippers' bodies and the journey here —
Newark headblown and still lights gathered.

Flew with buck eyes
Dermalogica spritz and loose kelp.
Balled-up polymide, layers of it.

A woman across the aisle said, look: Airforce One.

Get here please or some such hint
is a near-strong wish of
any aspect of anything.
    It's thrown a whole meter
        in the next slowdown 'will-get-better-if'
i.e. Lauder Shimmering Shield, unneeded.

It's for the cellular better

gradual life, gradated life   unsullied lidless abundant (the face, eyes wide).

Who put the slickering sound

into the room?

Monitory, perfidious.

2 |

Unlike the idea of travel.

Like him/her.

Like a hunted certain idea

minutely there but not enough.

OUTERING

Basso continuo

canon looping

ratio A major dominant

B minor submediant

note "blue for alice"

sounds the gap

of entering edge

& trailing edge of air.

Satellite Osumi burned up in '03. Numb sidling creature.

A shadowcone

on the sometime

perigee or apogee

wherever it is

the elliptic sits.

Wrong circuit type: was it a tether/tundra/killer?

or an escape craft

ambit strain away, thin filament.

I am sure, though, I saw it static stayed lightly quivering east-to-west, synchronous with us

an analemma in the sky

appearing in the thought-up angle

between orbit's vector and band of solstice.

A way to equinox is the 8

unitless

like a mug tilted turned twice.

Hear its phasing —

round rota sumer is icumen in.

THE FREIGHT

Soundsilt thrown so very far

and wide, hot as iron or icelike, who knows.

                    While travelling

I hear a car chase from N.Y to Ohio is emptiness.

Sun key a beam

to dotanddash

pretaught code, where are you, tell me.

An eddy of warm air means nothing.

Just the bend of waves.

                        Just matter boiling up there

in the corona, a quiet noise storm.

This is how my mind does.   It rotates in a passageway

the socalled "dorsal stream"   the "where" or "how"-way place in everyone's head. What I hear is murmur ha

see some losses

some language

see curved mirrors

throw sand back

several feet high, call, uncall

re-bound words

to particle, parallel waste:

∂hreibh, ∂ribanan —to mean dry no sorry "drift" —to mean—what you are driving at/driven to?

Stammer shutterlid, that's what and why

a new cell has 1 volt, just a small one.

Why all freeways are white and all tollbooths are home.

Look at the ground instead, then.   Look down for me

look at this new ground of mine.

ERRATA

The exhibition contains sixty-three manuscripts, including working drafts and typescripts of the first book; first editions of other work; and a trove of letters between the writer and his wife; his brother; his patron; and his fellow writers including 1, 2 and 3. These can be found in the adjacent room. The bulk of the collection covers the writer's early years through the publication of the second book. Pages from the third book are also here, fragmented. Found at the time of the writer's death, at the home of his brother, this collection was purchased for public view in 1958.

•

my ideal state is alone in some kind of offseason establishment   buffing, sloughing, tinting and when hot enough to go out, cool down slightly, then repeat. I'm white with a tinge of yellow, have a high luster, very malleable—talking all day of the same, the same old

   star moment of someone else, a man's hour, a man too remote to be arrived at

the phrase *auxiliary you* comes to mind, and *home is not far/careful of the head*

these things [are] mute, all weighed/veiled/vailed   Ah me, stop right now, I will be

a stark sterile, stark rarified thing if I keep this up   What language is that? Read it, there's a D., an Em, an
Ear to the…letters to read in a lapsing hot pale day

ἀσκός=luggage

someone says   "I'd have brought pot but we flew"

•

the depths I ask/of ask   does it say that?

A phrase: "America was made by you or those like you"

easing out, me outbrightened

not listening

flashing antlers/outlets/anothers   Which??

flights of great zeal   (this a clearer line)   *shamefully envoiced*

•

how irregular: couldn't read the long word *complet/textendcomplet*   but did see

Neglect the baying/? Beginning

and *Vain questions curl the hair how?*

•

What I know is that

June will come down sheet-ways,

great reaches of heat ending then starting

and the bed where I eventually lie, a cave, cava

—tine/time? The efficacy of prayer if you have/had?

will make no difference

In the whirring, heeling pulse beat, no-one will come

ἐξισχύω=enough

•

and I sat buffed tinted and waited

for the white car, a strange underjaw of doubt-feeling, nor my limbs so evened brown: room over-aired. *pretty pretty pretty*

well waited charred snarling in the head and with hope

there for two days without anyone else

Wrong palace/mixes nefarious (?) *maniac/quakefy* (written too small) *Terribly* (in pencil)

ἀποσπείρω=I shall see

•

Other Greek words: Broad. Arrow. Whatever. Station. Gratis. I take on/out. Not sure what you were expecting. *Skin irritant besides evilly imputed grace.* The cold like nothing else on arrival. J-peg for company when I left. A bladebone in the side of sense took 4 states out of me. How I missed these words in the house where I ended, and the bed I laid eventually.

Minola? No. *Miniscule to off.* ? WHAT? alleviate/emigrant. *If all well to know is half the ease*

| 13

there is blame, then.

OSCILLATE/OSCITANCE

                                    gutterperch/ballata

gauze tempering   bad earth   non-conductor

between is

        some third thing, some medium, said James Clerk Maxwell

and William Crookes found a luminiferous ether

                                        the subtle substance

14 |

for his radiometer

and its crack of cerusite/lead/metal vanes

[black on one side, bright the other]

coherer [heart]

                transmitter [bone]

the history of sound travel is namely death

but in a name: zinc wire coil

what you are hearing now is NOT my voice,   said Bernard Shaw/said Goethe   [through a machine]

a remodelled throat in a room caught the traces of me

in right & left swing of a needle —

                              scratch you write you restore

            in person   that person

circuit, circuitous

                        the larynx will only

admit the frequency escaped from it.

It says "not here"

NEVER SAW SO MUCH FIELD

Lightbundle convergence

stemming out & back

to a limit or *lim*

that's how I value it.

Dioptra with a scope at each end

could once screwcut

tunnels for aqueducts

measure stars

through ionized gas

& see sound   (act of the same)   as a radius of a curve.

How is it that lines of force must end

how a wave must swing like a pendulum

in harmony or else

there is loss of eddy current

per phase

per pole.

What is the new instrument.

What am I missing.

ANODE HAIL

Try to put this out, it will matter less and less.

Say celestial   say disc   say switch

say the extension is ugly

as is the O.C

as is covenant.

                    Gas station at five corners

magnolia dog, oat sky

land given to industry.

                              Think copper wires at the edge of a sea

and what they bring from the interrim, the interstice.   Anyone. Any.

And—as bad as it sounds—a telling, a forecast.

Area Code: John Wayne Gacy

reaching this point/he sees that he has written pain for paint   and it works better

(Tom Raworth, from 'South America')

along the way, it was. Inveigled in a hymn. Listen because that is the way I mean it   a hymn or a column.
List of the small, the onlys. Keys, tie, chocolate, my wife, Miami, a photo in the glove box: sons. There's
a maiming to work out. I went desolate and rich to a hotel/church thing last week. Anselm of Canterbury
says the mind, beyond right knowing, is lesser. Lesser than the feel of the new-sawn, the flowering of soap in
wood, all those envelopes unopened, the stagger and drag, arm bent back in the absolute day, shaving

in light that assailed, half-sleep riven by a torch. In another country, what is the mark of terror? Ligaments of
tow, a tightening of the bandwidth of the eye, every long unlettered blue vaporous thing to hoard. Not all the
fireflies weaving signs made it easier. By that I mean the time spent. Look at my body, the maguey surface of
it, its set-end color

I can still hear the soft crack   the seaming at the wrist. These days I've learned to see the event, the woman
downstairs, she brought a baby home, it cried, there was a treadmill at some point, the figure in the film I
made up a-flit from door to wall, don't stop that's perfect, I want it just there, there. Nearly bought a marble
table. Bad bad bad. Sometimes on the freeway things were momentarily pure and good, though. It was
always low to rain from a slate madstone sky

and here's an idea, barely there at the time   how certain symbols count. Dogs have followed me ever since,
their sutured mouths remote. The phrase 'you search for a home but you have one' is always never quite
right to be written, and it's not about this anyway. I never had a milk jug when I arrived and somehow that
has stayed with me. In Anselm's theory, a first cause the self-causing cause is repeated so perhaps

in sixty seconds a mistake over again, just a crack, might have been meant. Hair like a slash of canebrake or some other plant, restive, silken. All the while thinking of my first house, which it was, and the weird floor slant so the water came in. Canted and veering every day, a slow swing like my own hand, lifted

doing what I wanted, then drawn back. Neighbors let me see the underground, knocked in the closet-style hallway, said they're all walking home, everyone across the river. After that just a few coincident twists is all I need for something to assume the greatest importance. Empty shells, owlcalls. New clothes. Distance, says Anselm in the mind from what it tries to enact is for answer in whatever we make

or heal with science, solder a beloved thing with binding wire, wire gauze, wire pliers. I type equations: watts+feet+M %loss. I like the word fricative. Last week at the church at the very back, where-else, the walls came like a dip-net closedown and I fell out, I really fell. There were dog tracks, it was snowing and yellowish

and Anselm says the bad we are is known with inductive reason. Like a battery or effect of it, strange ghost of it, the slow spin of cells, the eventual snap-to. A silent downstroke on skin already cut. You the sum of the line of the point not there. A shining in me always sullen, you shine. Shine sullen, shine dissolved, shine sullen.

It's the repetition makes me a man. I was ill as all hell and you're likely not dead. There's a naming to work out, so many items like the rose aroma, and where a table should be 7, 8 feet away, blue leadlight window, the oldest tree on the street. Prayer, water, ipecac, the salve and the bitters of it. Many-spined ideas, they crawl. I lived there for quite a while.

Memo

VOLMET tells who is   Who transmits from what origin who uses number stations

who is the morse or voice, in whip antennae linepass

anonymous recipient who are you I speak to does it matter

what is it the word Attention then a bell or gong shotwave numbers

your pattern of iotas each phrase has an equal number of these iotas

they are binary to make matters worse   an automated voice

come here

a brief once

uttering 2 times

the repeat

tells you to land —as aircraft or —in the upper sideband or —to

divide the planet up in *volmet*, in a hangland, in modulations:

double-sideline supressed

double-sideline reduced   AM   QAM quadrature amplified and   OPPOSITE

OPPOSITE

O   Ohm (electrical resistance)   SIGMET (significant meteorological)

        large hail, dust, sand, so much sand

        laboratory sand,

in the sky

a SQUALL LINE

HE-CHILD

In He-Child's case there was some offensive things. Scaramande played, glass shards, a credit card, leaves on the cat carpet, underwear, small and floral, slipping, brothel creepers. He lived among a vacant lot, dulled and ireful. Unroadworthy car outside, its seats split. "Belliqueux" he showed me. I am irascible, that's the extent of his French. Most remembered:

I had to mend the bulb on the landing and the frescoes on the wall.

In a pulp story (1955) 'La Scottoline' winds her hips.

Ellipsis parameter and error.

On the bone-spoon color of the main drag here, a hotel lying wide fully paved, new.

If you press me, you'll hear the soughing/sifting of worlds, pure cipher/

unsurpassable. An answer won't come (I want to add "to one in crisis") but I do have the odd line; this one —

"bring my city back, my back my witness" over and over again, I'm sure it'll fit somewhere.

Like the time on Euston Road when the phrase "diamond synchrotron" made me think of him, and in my head it somehow meant "are you happy in your work, are you happy?"

Dead pristine soulless diamond lastend, I wrote later. I'm mouthing it now and I say

"I know you. You get bored easily. I know you in your airless room and your hats hung up

lax and hunched, unmoving not unhappy. Johnny Rotten called you "killer dog" once,

in that place where trains run underfoot. In Za-Za lounge you ordered a Gibson

and got a gimlet, and I'd got a back-edging slice to the head and went mad—thought I saw

Demetrius from AMND in flight over the gorge, even madder". How these scenes spill.

Of which, there are pails on the driveway for water.

I could have sworn I heard a radio downstairs, but no.

LAG

jewellery/jewelry (depends)

soft food/paraffin/—dark vinegar

ruinous roll walk   dead-end guyed pole

on the tracks, trains don't go/knot me/kilo me—

ter/or me   I have to end somewhere, a

pharmacy/chemist/ how *you're*

too ambitious   said woman on the way

it's a recoil of disruptive discharge

what are you doing out

on steatite roads-crumbling-

fade-into-storm-valley of four corners

soak it out residual   /it's all yellow here

and this the only hill

snap/switch   loop the plier

plastic bag move-able

through a long run/should be   taped

hook of a snake   felt in the neck

—shunt motor breeze,   —it's coming

mainline-as-not-yet/not yet

core pins on the ground

globes silver cyanides   silicon bronze

on a bar-room table/odd how cheap

raceway is a metal casing

electrolier is to hold up incandescence

the house I live in now is so called/

and made on account of that

---that &   its hysteresis (loops plotted, cycle curves

waste waste waste)

SQUALL LINE

[July 26, 2005. On this date a manyscaled front moved eastward over Lake Erie, the lake being 4-5 °C cooler than land. Thunderstorms before a drier mass. Strong wind. Rising motion of an arcus cloud, or 'shelf cloud'—

a dark horizontal band. Dustgraze on its rim, turbulent on the underside]

That women—

kinematics: motion of objects

without asking why they do so

That a storm passes   hot air into the updraft--imagine red arrow—where rain-cooled air—imagine blue arrow—slips in the downdraft. Leading/outer edge a gust front   sudden wind change with it   lateral wind a downburst—imagine water striking flat surface—it leaps in disparate streams—throws out—so much—so many.

That a squall line

is a downburst creator

in warm season

& that day was warm.

A high dewpoint near the shoreway

pre-storm close & tight, spraymantled skin, house unimportant.

When convex heat binds with cold

there is a change in kinematics

unascertained trajectory: the *bow echo*

the arc compact in a squall line.

Enhanced inner winds/rear notches/quickbands.   It moves parallel to front

its atoms repeat & pulse in radar return

in bay-gaze to long distance.

A throwback/a dark strata/a cumulous.

A ragged mass of scud/fractals

small eddying & no margin.

N. Taylor Road 0121-0208 CST
Thunderstorm Wind (EG55)
Cleveland Heights
Strong gradient gusts ahead 40 knots (46 mph)
ahead of a
deepening surface low and approaching squall line.

Likely
damage from the bow echo segment.
Some pause before event.

•

Women push onward into an empty city

in the hours of three to four

wronged & golden

careering through terrible heat

in a baseless patrol.

Limbs in a mid-pounce.

Saying

in a take we have come to see you   this man   this event.

Come to see you

on the gravel, at the door

in the walls

our eyes through slats—

the plicae of pale wood

skewed by a dry wavebreak of missing.

Eddy Road 0105-0230 CST 40k
Thunderstorm Wind (EG55)
E. Cleveland
Awning sheared off a gas station
along with a sign and antennae
blown over.

& if you look back at us, you will see
we are the screen flashing up lightly
all your bad ways.
A parade that never wearies—
the aspersion, the scattering
of ourselves cast

& if you should look back again

Ask, How do you stand with me?

We'll stay the lungs of your house

our voice in a laminar flow, repeating

Euclid Ave. 0240-0312 CST 70k
Thunderstorm Wind (EG55)
E. Cleveland
All power lines blown down.
Swath of 70mph wind.

We are harder than you think, we are harder.   Who are you

but a fix? We met you in parking lots & hotels —

Units, limits

able to be told, and you did

in long-lived bowing lines—in ink—on your arm—

our names—so long & how we lost—

E.105 St. 0314-0357 CST 70K
Thunderstorm Wind (EG55)
Glenville
Power lines down

•

| 33

I moved along

with the rest of them

up from the flats

by Conrail Bridge

where red light beats over

the shoreside ends

& arches every half hour.

Through wide underpass galleries

all to cram you back into your skin

to say—What is it about you?

To become the dust

in the garden, a grainy disquiet

To say—

We will come to mind, now, stirring

like a dissolve in transit

like a dream you had

of pylons lying on the street

of a petrol slick inch-to-

-inch downtown

of a book in this socalled dream

that I & we should walk in newness

in a solid echopoint in a spill

in a phrase

heard on the interstice of thought.

Look at the sky, see the bitter it shares.

How it all passes for you

a cirrus raft claddrifted footpad

as you sleep fully dressed

E. 73rd St. 0400-0600 CST
Thunderstorm Wind (EG55)
Erie
Several homes had the tin
pealed off the roof along
with shingles
pealed off others. Wood

sidings of some buildings
broken. Trees uprooted
and many power lines. One
unconfirmed fatality after
small conflagration.

drop into the room below

as if into the lake

of which nothing.

Nothing more but a squall line, a preface to the letting-in
                    To the letting-in   To your space   To the moment   When I say

Get on your hands to me

On your knees

edge left, right   through sand piles cut with halite

Like a film in its frame-to-frame workings

or your dust jackets

that melt into colored, cacaphonic dread

Past the cymballs in the sink

tendering, left by someone,

& typing ribbon on the floor —

It shows the restless whip of your life

& how the clouds-in-clouds outside

must remind you of layers, scores, subtexts,

what you could have said   Said in several ways

or in perfect reverse This? Is the lot of us

A number for what   for one after the other

for what?

                    Deep-drowning faces

tattooed on a shoulder

In a column

In the hold of a held pattern where

I am the last one in

        & I will reel you down

where this mad scene falls

  For the house is on fire

       & the ceiling pleats over us

It's that place of blanched variety, first of dream

said *no coastline the frontage road.*

Winter solstice occurs at the instant when the Sun's position in the sky is at its greatest angular distance on the other side of the equatorial plane from the observer's hemisphere,

lengthening nights and shortening days.

The band of the zodiac *zōdiakos kuklos* is always at an oblique angle. Solstice fr. LL *sol* and *sistere.* Inter —

it can fall in the middle or end or start the world as I know it again —

cold backdrop aerial coil, sky miasma.

And allbeing said is first of dream, where the frontage road is very real, most real

dug back in now and up, day moulting off

yes, how it stains. Blued-on-concrete, shadow-of-the-east.

                        And allbeing said who else

has edges this keen?   who dreams as me?

evergoing wheelsleet cross-bind

country —

        girl whose

lowly ties mean I can't be at church.

Supposedly empty is the beginning of all things

and troubled is this body

its hollow stairstep face.

LULL

light here instinctual

uncanny then eureka

various props

mirrorous

silica strung

wetly walled in

poolbench tiered

sick grid glow

a vainglorious, pretty

pretty pretty

much blood weary

scene america

flat plain imagined

though arterial

PATROL

for g. emil reutter

stood up, waist having thickened

uneven and cleverer

betook of revolution nightly, patter fit

steps upswing market street, termini

time cinched and biding, lots of time

a grief spell lifted, thought to be something else

in this bad frame philadelphia, shiver seeming

wide undiagrammed

where new year is borrowed

and the psychics' mail is most unread

Specular, 6 p.m.

So very closed
lucent
a shock
a shock
though insentient
is to the end
a bluing
freezing fasted time

143

of a body an alias
a knot shuteyed blind the moment I know
and I know the name of who inside that
knot of modules is a body
its shale pared away
to get smaller, to get closer
in a long time
in a shock
in its end, stopped short
to cut a decent figure in the world, to be pure
to pare away inchoate
and be light
light as achrome thought.

SMALL AIR

Antioch Hotel

where trains pause in the lobby   a strange attractor for debris

blanched

airpocket hotel its

bodies fall to the street

in a guttering flock

& you not caring a voice

is thrown from the walls always

you besieged, besieged.   Hear the name Antioch/Antakya

how the museum recast that lost

ancient city & all you could do

was sit & drink in

the bar: called Halite Bar   the rim of a glass salty

& think of halite rock

its concoidal fractures millionfold

a seam beneath you.

Stare, drinking   hear   how the crusader Princes of Antioch were emptytitled in the end.
How the Antioch Chalice was not used at the Last Supper.

•

            If you sink an object in Lake Erie
it will emerge beaded, a bonediamond.   Someone's skull a spiderweb, imagine —
hard as the pavement trace of white outside
        & downtown shuttered, its
centre all dug out & instead

a countercross/score of limbs/lines on the

real skyline &   numbness   a numb pale scoria lifting/falling

& still so hard   that Antioch, Ohio

was the last same place before now. And you sat in the same way, same hotel

    in the vitreous   luster   of you   (yourself, sitting)

in a lean-to room   with a touchup and half-grey smile —

(What a battle what a bad winter a bad journey)

To vacant shapes in rocksalt   cordless faces on the wall.

Aporia Poem

1. Délire de negation.
2. Deliquescence   dissolving of.
3. Sinusoidal current free of polar effect.
4. Negative cell with spongy surface usually of a color.
5. Warm coil (spiral gearing).
6. Smell of copperas/ferrous sulphate/green vitriol.
7. Iron pyrite in the air, then.
8. core, core and shell, cored carbon, coreless armature.
9. lady lazarus.
10. dec —
11. Tem to Temu (entrails buried elsewhere).
12. Soap on gums (lamictal).
13. Posturing more (lithium ion silvering).
14. Set the fire alarm off twice (clozapine 300mg).
15. Pyramids and Palm Trees test 50/54. Normal.
16. Corsi block span one or two less than digit span, low.
17. Say *cogito* without *ergo sum* again.
18. Merely a pause, properly so-called.
19. Self-formula, unary.
20. Shale pared away, a jigsaw in reverse.
21. All foveae fallen. Hymen ruptured?
22. Well-kempt and rather sleepy.

Bravura Cool

Immersion braze is to dip a thing in solder (a feasible alloy, tin and lead) and flux (limestone or chalk). Hold the thing in the fire a little while to heat. When it is lowered into the solder, the latter will flow into the joint and firmly attach itself. Before dipping, the thing to be brazed is coated with a special anti-flux graphite, covering all the surface except that which is to be brazed.

Pares itself with a drawknife.

Reacts along the hallway, back and forth

Trailing spelter, un-set a stream of it.

Run down cell, fitting, spent hours

Hours on the shelves, for ages, tidying.

Some injury. Pity the snow fell so soon.

RADIOSÉANCE

-for Tom McCarthy

i.

Agraphia the lack of power to write; in my last report there was a poem

Certain as a day, a day cry halt to what—what did it really mean?

Called obsidian drift.

Now about feeling.

| 49

It came through the instrument. On that subject

Can you see me sitting the other side of you?

See yourself raddled in a beautiful light. Heavily clad

Like a plane for take-off. Engine cowl, souter hanged.

Can you hear that noise?

An ice on stove impression.

ii.

A reach to a difference of subtler type. Differential coil, a part of a current flowing though unknown resistance, the other part flowing through the known. Differential compound wound dynamo. A dial driven home. A hide for more than a moment.

Neither death nor life nor height nor depth:

Aeternumque adytis effert penetralibus ignem: from the everburning flame comes

sanctuary. Sensate, sensate, I got on far the best when conditions were right

when the room was hot, a permeate slide

through skin hot wood another hot space.

When I died in the world, and elapsed you all

between the waking and the going deaf.   I left my hands as they were

re-tied, having

strong thought from some quarter. Intent from it

I looked up.

I made the shadow and the wall draw back.

iii.

What bulk can we ascribe to signals? Are they small large long fluid straight circular

a fix a star-map, just an old code.

Give a meaning.   You see

Aboulia is the loss of will, or the will to. Through a limestone wall, will it place on me a wind

will I hear you? Do I believe you?

Resistance slide: something cutting in or out of

a circuit. Opposition from a substance or body

to the passage through it. Opposition to the impulse

or pressure of another force. Resistance of the

air to a body. Body an arrow a lag a lull

a stream. Air blanched air

the rip in its closed design is a mouth opening.

Resistance is the dark reciprocal of conductance.

iv.

Suffering in the corridors

the red lamp is signal and prolonged waiting

taptap

wave draws past like a blanket

tears a line from a phoneme, a whisper
from a diode

as I glide interfrequenz

hiss: "now"   for the ultrashorts of a speech   vibrating

murmur ha do you hear? Get me the blank spot between stations. Put me

in a Faraday cage
tinfoiled

—I will still scratch you in   automata *durch Radio*

in diverting

hurried scraps

someone has trouble in throat/tonight as you think

of /inter/intake/irregular/removing/a test spin

a stretch of low/through slight wires/imminent

nonlinear/best best best wire/of my life/slicing

| 53

Our studio our studio teasing small ecstasies   *Pero sigue con los tratamientos para la sangre*

(continue the treatment for your blood)

v.

by lesion

of cerebral

centers

for speech

Aphasia

when you cannot sense it

onceloved thing

in vocative

lull

a misnomer

in a hole

is my own

no real time behind a scene

just aphasic

telephasic   crossed-over

penwork a misfire

   —telautograph

from the site

of a sender   sp/ac/ial

me-/ac/ou/stic

stuttering already a/buzz underphrase

tu/l/pe   gai/sa/!   th/e tu/lip is/bri/ght

di/ode

          too/ha/rd pa/rt/ed

vi.

Mouth shut by rags: *Aphonia* the incapacity to utter, breathe

or eat or drink   The god of my town   you say   will unwind me, exchange

me   Encored, stuck in something so small   as a papercut in space

the invisible hingejaw of a switch

vii.

Polyglot

this trial   *Insufficient residual magnetism*

From

a device shut, cued/a (continuum)

a pavilion (ear) a horn (mouth)

A once-eared place, not a one-horsed dawn (horse a radio) Who beat the loud-

sounding

Heel of a boot   die die and then she said words like

"DIMORPHISM", "DIPOLAR"

"*dii-consentes*, the twelve, *conserentes*, gods"

so many gods no call for them

"ði-inferes, ði manes"

meaningless meaningless

die is an attempt at the name/the automatist laughed, "not a one-horsed dawn"

laugh being an echo of what was meant

and got reproached   or die-words   a crash-thought stuttermerged/emerged

and the automatist forgot, sorry didn't hear, sorry didn't write it

but mainly that

our great dead all the same/retain their sense

and how I shall be exiled (written down)

      "exiled"

                                        This is an awful day, to pass

                                        To pass

Over/saw it all, overheard hidden

in cleft of canopic space, echoic space

waiting for a word

all meanings

coagulant

automatist tongue

a cloverleaf

crossmodal

insofar that

nameless is

the breathtakeknowing no/thing

ethercaught

nameless is you

the conduit closed over

SLEW RATE, CURVED NOT BINARY

Usual day, long drop to it, the very edge of which
data that talks, breaks and bleeds

says *all else is deleterious*.

That's a phrase that came here before morning

but much of it has vanished now
through hours of imbalance, the best part of hours

to some recordable form
a dinning, jagged thing

so write it down only it's always
gone on its way, into

the left-tilt of a letter, turning counterwise.

God here a slipcase on occasion

sometimes useful, sometimes not.

Iʙ/Bᴀ

Nunavut: the opening of the mouth

a terrain in the north, "our land"
or your land

dawn chorus canada, hey Saturday sun

Nullity: deadend, in fetter of sheets
a space where your real name
your language gets lost
in sleepily dead, the terror of great sleep
is a mouth close by death, fluidly drifting

unswathed, untied

                      by settlers

                      by priests

who leave confusion

One-spa/two-spathe cannot speak "space"/come to light

incrementally

recollectible

is the gold

boat widening over the head (from your land to mine)

Faring tongue can now stutter

out of absence

      into a middle

      an interval

and say amentia, beautiful word

      how a message cannot get through

amentia: a lack

or lag when your real name is lost,

itinerant, inert

in cosmography in symbol

in a passageway   *(area of primal breakdown between)*

Of breakdown

SHALL CEASE AND BE AS WHEN, SEPARATE AND DRIFT

Can of sweet potato I ate—against a radiator. Bowmore, Bloom wine, indolent.

Slow remains on my eyes—the path of every loping animal around.

How precise can I be.

Run of girls on highway 9.

Beheaded, I hope. The whole lot.

One day, just one, let them see me.

I will use them

As a clock, and hold them to each.

Let them see.

Halfway/Substance

Polarity can be seen in a crystalline subject, i.e. if a quartz is pressed it is electric for days

the piezoelectric effect

a throw of potential sent   across all its faces.

Crystal detectors of iron pyrite

                                        they are a oneway thing, i.e. they change

alternate waves to

        an elastic staggering pitch

of sound silvering   limberly perceived.

•

Makeup of quartz crystal: general forms of hexagonal prism with each end mounted by a hexagonal pyramid. Each crystal has three principle axes 1). Z or optical axis (negative temperature coefficient) 2). X or optional axis (positive temperature coefficient 3). Y or mechanical axis.

In a XY cutcrystal it is possible to have two resonant frequencies close together. The amount of current that can pass though a crystal ranges from 50-200 milliamperes. For very high frequencies the crystal must be very thin and easily broken. You can grind a quartz plate to operate higher.

•

....halfway bear down

on a crystal tourmaline

skew symmetrical, all its plains

a needletop   littleset

clear, pellucid. Silica in a form you can tell

in a tinier form

where I cool I solid

into several beautiful means

to silver nitrate in fluid

to another silver, crystals of glass. Into glass, silica strung

like Baily's beads

the skinning of a nebulae

as the moon passes by. In shards a line of a circlerift, dying circular.

Each word

a crystal in carbon, in sky.

Arc-lasting.

Oscillating

but always in the same place.

HALFWAY/CIRCUMNAVIGATE

strayed lines and geometric

out of Euclidian world world

into neural nucleus of body

units fastbroke down

feed on you covet you all

neutral actions turns to

a code a rebus a letter you

put a wire sadly by the

sea for me exactitude where

purport must be the brain

is all wrong its basal ganglia

and sockets whiling away

in *lim*erence the otherword

for starving quartz cold and

where the first minute was flexing silence

how I knew before the crosswind hit

Halfway/Feeling

Got to get to

what gives the land its play of force —

the force draught

  land unfractured   taken up and

easing to a blear day   day made from the sea

in swishpan of eye, tense fainting eye

     and what is here is

     the history of glass. Georgius Agricola who saw its

     slow unvectored move

     to the shore

     the crystal obsidian.

Fulgurite hard and tall from lightning

sandtumbled aerials

unselective untuned   radio on the beach.

Signals drawn off in quicklime   phosphorus   shellac   silicon.

Fine-mesh flat dream of space

aquaria flat visioned.

A body can fall through this. Body an old stellar type.

Angled to a line of firebolts

with a wild turn from the neck   foreshortened in midair.

Every unclaimed fibril—

—chamfered—silently—mad—and shards

tripdarting—diagonal

in the whole
non-rayed non-wrinkling
hush-now still-now sky.

Halfway/Stasis

I have many ideas for you   it's time to meet

in this room I have

its color is very odd

torn like animals, half-apart and reversed

grey/pink, grey to pink how I hate it all

a morphed coral gullied absence of talk

and I'm glad you turn up   with your great confidence

as if you could predate the moon

or buy me a new head

but I don't know where   your "viscera of the moments"

came from, nor do I

know the limbic system, its belt between what and what

I want to say it is the simple standing

in a kitchenette

the water cold and totally silver.

A fight. A noise.

Because you'd driven off, down a caving stem of road.

"Caving stem"   being

the brain being

what you think I think.

LOQUELA

Speak you:

The world has a visibility greater than six miles.

What is this winter that doubles in weight and reels —

Stony ochreous sun and the hard —

Start again: How do you feel when I say

there is something terribly wrong in these windows?

It means there is cylinder oil in my mouth

there is murder somewhere, brake-block, break

the head [dement, dent] in grey chipped room.

For what for what, should I say

exculpate? Sun is not ochreous

no, is gone to a cry a high

unnoticed weft. It changes hour to hour.

How do you feel, how do you stand with

me? I'll not say exculpation. Why, it's a

mistake I put my face to

and say no, or dear dear, I didn't

like walking in that building

at night, the corridors my heels

white black check, white one two

body accordioning, breathe—

and the wait—

How it spilled

and spilled, how I let

be unfolded the life I unfold, still do

in a strange restive outpost

a leaflike bract of a town. We hallucinate it back.

It gangles up it grabs the face, alleviates

in yes or no, there's no sense of measure

but the enchantment is there

and I lose you I lose you in that

in that the speakers (those in me) always return the tone.

DRIVING TO DEC~

delta-like outpost

south of here

sun spathe on fields

deciphered at last

dear nothing, dear prayer

more scantness

grid of little displaced

there was audience, there is brave

like a microscope or roulette

we escaped but can't

go and everyone knows

AREA CODE: MONA VAN DUYN

The   car   has   run   over

—loosesleet ground, loosening yet another loss—

has run over something. Think formula   formula   formula
get out spinelit on W.3rd, feel the crickle of nerves from a sensor on-off, on-off
and look down at a body crouched like a held note, immobile
sliding pigment-wise into the snow.

Come closer, who is it what is it. Light a cigarette at its base
watch it recede and blame me away (though it was never there).

Drive home, frighten myself up. Think: *formulaformula: be quiet*
(though the contours of the throat are hammered out).
There'll be a phone call afterwards, and usual guilt/ fear/not-fear/fear.

It's the matter of it I hate. The door wide open, couch two feet to the left, gauze in the sink.

If I see you again, I'll hang you with glass.

You accident, so tacit, unthinkable.

FIND POEM

Field Manual: Marginals, Disconnects, Semaphores, Indecipherables.

Notes Towards.

Poem tracks (in brackets) Ideas collaged with Information Gathered. Also unused

e.g. Comb lightening arrester/gaps between

(*think this*) like teeth of a comb. Freeway. Inter—etc. Inter/state. Interstate ||

The gap/the caesura/in the difference/the intake of breath/the rupture/the intermission. Wrists cut, limbs lopped.

Verdigris: strange ghost of it. Green crystal on the terminals of a battery/Voltaic Arc: the source of light in an arc; bow shock or arc of brilliant light between two conductors/heat produced is so intense that the space is filled with vapor/it carries the current across. Vitriol.

[a hunted certain idea

in trace of a non-room

in its non-corners]

auroral storm/a sheet/stream/streak of

wan fire.

[a north-

fleeting

waste-strait

winterish, magnetic

pressure leak from the car

all over the gravel]

/Magnetine OR magnetic creep (increase of force

in a body

being magnetized/galvanized). Also called 'time hysteresis'.

I think surveillance is 'magnetic observing'.

Cerusite: carbonate of lead used for crystal detectors

CRYSTAL RECTIFIER

(a radio device comprising two crystals resting against each other to balance the incoming signals).

[& one time

I imagined you me god

& the weather on a road

cut in four

like there were four ways]

Glass/mirror/murmur. Glass cannot insulate wire. It collects a film of moisture

during hightension transmission. Volume and entropy in glassmaking, its slow creep. Obsidian drift.

Loss. Loss of. Let me see. Corona loss: when 2 wires (with difference of pressure between) are placed close together. 'Loss' takes place at critical voltage (corona outer atmosphere, faint is its light).

Corona is showed by radio emission//the corona can refract and scatter radio waves—it has an occulting disc/

A mirage all in the wrong place. Burning ships in the sky/sky on the road or desert.

          Corona has irregular clouds, through which small bright radio stars

          Become diffuse/Are cut off

for 20 days. In their path along a perimeter of space. Think of a satellite train

   lagging   a body in its disintegration

[and this is in no way a love song or a myth]   made so out of solitude…..

COULD NOT

No, I'll read again, but not "this" or "this"

                   where I hoped to fall in and be quite unlike myself

and after "that" the deep of silence certain.

(science the problem that's what I say

what was in and out--

with...............................? what was allowed)

Though I can't tell

        can't tell what it was

of "that" I indexed

from gazework, from subsets, from the sheer unbearable (of not having it).

Oh you christian daughters

of sorts, all of a series, dishonesty.

I'm your best best killer who kicked you up twice and more

and I never told you why "The Return" was typewritten, could only have been.....

WHOSEES

1.

The eye is a long steady-state/ threatening eye

Untutored
unable to blink

If it could
then the house is a door
    is a port, a mere slit
warp thread
porta fenestella

with a spindly god to show the way

2.

Seeming error soulmost error
And the error is logic

that seemed so right and will be right when the house

is not a collection of sorts

new formica / drawer liners/the one chair—leather

its tiny catch at the skin

and the seeming immobile hang

a kind of evening delay

shadows aft-edging on a smooth

flat of wall

agreements left and the watching for them

3.

That the house is a door, is a shade.

Is a non-contract

opening

and should never open to show

as that would be what happened

4.

In the accident/a slack hollow

a mind let go to dumb working-

jaw kind of silence

lost away into graven awful peace lost

life

deep into anechoic deep/backdrifting inner sound

      someone

condensed by quietude

static and foundered

5.

Tree house

skin-stretched dun road house

Rapier road with a house breathing

Propeller fan box fan

6.

A swerve

a blurred out slow phase

the end of this/the end of that/haphazard

      difficult to tell which

on the intersection crossed like a smile bite

wheels like blood raying in full swing

An updraft of dense ions

And red from a receding thing is redder in color than when approaching

Running leaving the approaching the

Doppler effect a lackslip of thought

for a second

Sidelobe sound of night animals

7.

In a house once

routed from downtown on rollers

       over timber

the mural shot with capillaries

faulting out to each end corner

Message artifact house

made and spaced in real bodies

those who take the days known only to them

8.

Behind a shutter lid

time so wasted, way back

Time of watching cars

their surge, their suck

and a mini-storm

its water left in pans for the lawn

for the yard scalding

9.

A story house

an every scale house

Every hot fold

a roseboard aroma

unvocalized

the pale and flat bodies pass tight and tired as ever

    up to see a trap

in the attic and down

like floor-to-beam leaves at a kitchen window

desert plain to extramusical sky

10.

Buick skitched on gravel at 5.am

awake in scratchy blue fraying a blanket

the last few hours tapping at things. Dream: a man cut and culled from whale fat

or softening wood. And how old children wrote names there

over and again how the house is —

a madeover monster world in the heat that circles and mounts

a spasm of accident bad accident

sprawl and stupor

mapless

is a wait for aspartame tea

is dawn,

is a limber flick of leaves

the gradual dazzle of ceiling

11.

A skin scratching

when the light is blue and picked away

by remedies for boredom

How to swell in the heat that circles/ how to fill the space like a monster

tapping out what happened but

       too late

for the world shuddering back

through a trellis of the not-heard

the initials on the stairs from the children from the fire

       the hurried swoop down

through a softening door

soft back then

and now

a little lens

a nothing the revision

by a dark adapted eye

hateful lidded eye

12.

And what to do is to

think the house down as far as

the trapshell to grow in

fronded and sick

a vestibule

in which to prepare

13.

For

today out of three weeks

    has been very mundane

14.

Slicing up the formless /quietly slicing thighs

aching misordered

the rising from

a lying and sweating in doubt

> the fret

> the patrol

while styrofoam boxes curdle and film

> and in the head

there is slow burn and floodtide

a clagged banded world

told in scenes that spill before morning:

lips of whales cut back

a dead barge moved from one space to another

15.

And in the eye is a net

Dry-pieced and wide

as a house, sparing

in all the wrong way

its purpose laid out

clear a poor secret

such an accident

in water-burn

in the angle of

fore-and-back

in the surge the suck between

leaf patterns in the mute gleam of a window

where sleep

is inside

and where the blue sills hang

IN CASE OF NO CASE FOR MADNESS: BILOCATION

It seems to me you are managing

to come along good in your unfoldment. A forestall

from the mouth

                  sigla in

                  the skin, open core

                  link fuse

                  signspelling.

In your room close to the door, the middle shelf, take

the eighth book from the left; halfway down is a term

conveying to fall back or falter, I am sure on a page.

                              (this is what I looked for)

Rather more than halfway. Given with exact precision

and sure there it was

"…to whom a crucified Christ was a stumbling block…"

I chanced to be one time along the coast

it was 1914

and I heard the guns.

I chanced to be one time in a city

it was 2005

and I saw bodies fall from the sky.

ATLANTIC LUMEN HOUR

of fluxion

of lines

that run

through

       a cross-contact

cross-plane

      & between that

unstillness/wayward

for a short time only

         standard from incandescent

is a magnet—

      a lamellar magnet

where one face is east   the other west

& for a short time only   a spark/single

thin brilliant —

                    gapwire gauge light

so uniform from a candle falls in

                        pitchfall eventually

an event in

the start looping

to its partial stop

is not going

to help us now

what has happened has happened

Réseau *

......half way   halfway

of the west-to-the-west

haze-line striations

resemble tight spray

o december

re-laced, re-sewn

99

re-eve- to pass through a hole and back: a miniscule turn, a self-curve

the horizon a band

to move under, never long wet, never long dry

weather centre reads lo.   L.O.

sublunary   its coldlike breath   around itself a   white square on the window

where the glass is a chart

                    its finework the sky

far Draco, Auriga,

Lacerta, Serpens

Sagittari, Antares

A flat spindle sketch

take it away

hold it to the pull-blind light

that leaves the house so.

          Numeral. This to that. To that this. A trace

like birdseed, bright dots on a basin, a triptych times two.

And through it, the street

snow-bent, siftspill

white ever-ours

passes by

a tiny icedrift

cirrocumulus

undrawn

can't be drawn

immutable

in its mingling figure.

How it works in me, it leases   [lets out]   makes me say

yes, there will be precipitation tonight   [on the eaves] later mist slipping in airfoil chill

and o [l.o] the weather centre, its black stitch print

        is broken

in a halfway life

through a hole on a glass []

where L is half

or almost.

And I'm sure there was something in the road that fell from you or me.

An acrobat or a face.

A cirrus spill lid fall lid fall.   Just shy of one cloud.

In the lateness of the day, silvering gladly

I left prints in the snow to the neighbor's fence

dark incline run-off holes

diagrammic

point to point

pain vs. gravity

loosening space about me.

*Meshed ground in lace. *Astronomy:* a network of fine lines on a glass plate, used in a photographic telescope to produce a corresponding network on photographs of the stars. *Meteorology:* a system of weather stations under the direction of a single agency or cooperating for common goals.

GIVE

Held held held. You the bagged-up limbs in every hallway. It calls for blood, the calls are blood. It was around this time I started codifying and couldn't stop. Wickerwork everything. Got all razorous. Namely I'd have died if someone hadn't turned me over.

There was a war and I was against it. I'm sure some lines weren't there, and were added since. Some were about a sleeping woman, the sun across her dry hide. Some were about people on television, walking home across Waterloo Bridge after the underground bombs. One got scored out very quickly because I couldn't do it. Such as America is a cavatina, a canticle, or another nonsense phrase in the skitter and drift of 3pm dreams. How here a beat-out shape of an idea, a whiteblaze kind-of-settle. Old unsteadystate of hunger.

Enough. You should know I ran six miles today and afterwards held out my arms with the poise of a millionaire, maybe to add drama. It's like fernseed after fire, that's what I feel.

And you KNOW what this was all about. The need itself to say the "you were" the "you are" the *you are*. America no longer disorder, ruinous, awry.

Now rolled out flat, storied into, shone upon.

Just a moment first about my body. You see, it still does things in its telegrammic way.

NOTES

—'Oscillate/Oscitance' is inspired by the stories of Salomo Friedlaender (1871-1946) Auguste Villiers De l'Isle Adam (1838-1889) both of whom wrote about early sound technologies.

—'Area Code: John Wayne Gacy' refers to Anselm of Canterbury's conception of divine truths in *Proslogian* (1077):

Something than which nothing greater can be thought of cannot exist only [as an idea] in the mind because, in addition to existing [as an idea] in the mind, it can also be thought of as existing in reality [that is, objectively], which is greater [than existing only as an idea in the mind]. If something than which nothing greater can be thought of exists only as an idea in the mind, then "that than which something greater cannot be thought of" is "that than which something greater can be thought of," which is impossible [because it is self-contradictory]. Therefore, it necessarily follows that something than which nothing greater can be thought of must exist, not only as an idea in the mind, but in reality.

….In its most succinct form, is as follows: "God, by definition, is that for which no greater can be conceived. God exists in the understanding. If God exists in the understanding, we could imagine Him to be greater by existing in reality. Therefore, God must exist.

(St. Anselm's *Proslogion*. M.J. Charlesworth (ed.). Notre Dame: Notre Dame University Press, 1979)

—The idea for 'Squall Line' was generated by Guy Debord's film, *In Girum Imus Nocte Et Consumimurm Igni.* (1978): "we turn in the night and are consumed by fire".

—'It's that place of blanched variety, first of dream' borrows a line from the poem 'Pyramid' in Guillevic's *Geometries* (1967):

Who else has edges this keen?

Who is clear-cut as me?

And:

We simplify the world

The world offers itself

Our dream.

—'Specular 6p.m.' is inspired by the Austrian logician and philosopher Kurt Gödel (1906-1978) who developed fundamental ideas about axiomatic systems; showing that in any mathematical system there are propositions that cannot be proved or disproved within the axioms of the system. In 1977, he developed an obsessive fear of food and died as a result of extreme malnutrition.

—'Radioséance' owes its structure and event to F.W.H Myers's *Human Personality and Its Survival of Bodily Death* (1903). The "one-horsed dawn (horse a radio)" is a reference to Jean Cocteau's play of 1926, *Orphée*, and the film of the same name (1950). Cocteau initially introduced the horse as a device used to convey messages from the underworld (and also as a critique of automatic writing experiments by spiritualists and artists of the Surrealist movement). In the film, the horse is replaced by a short-wave radio that transmits individual lines of code-poetry to Orpheus from Cégeste.

—The allusions in 'Ib/Ba' are from *The Egyptian Book of the Dead*, specifically the concept of the soul: comprised of five parts: Ren (the name), Ka (the energy), Sheut (shadow) Ba (soul) and Ib (heart).

—In 'Halfway/Feeling' there is a reference to the German scientist Georgius Agricola (1494 –1555), an early pioneer of mineralogy.

—'Could Not' concludes with the title of Ezra Pound's poem 'The Return' (1912):

See, they return; ah, see the tentative

Movements, and the slow feet,

The trouble in the pace and the uncertain
Wavering!

See, they return, one, and by one,
With fear, as half-awakened;
As if the snow should hesitate
And murmur in the wind,
     and half turn back;
These were the "Wing'd-with-Awe,"
     inviolable.

Gods of that wingèd shoe!
With them the silver hounds,
     sniffing the trace of air!

Haie! Haie!
   These were the swift to harry;
These the keen-scented;
These were the souls of blood.

Slow on the leash,
     pallid the leash-men!

—Aspects of 'Whosees' can be attributed to Alan Robbe Grillet's novella 'La Jalousie' (1957).

ACKNOWLEDGEMENTS

Many thanks to the editors of the following journals in which several of these poems have appeared, sometimes in different versions: Blazevox, Blackbox Manifold, Cricket Online Review, Dear Sir, Fox Chase Review, Horse Less Press, La Petite Zine, Moria, Otoliths, Upstairs At Duroc and Vlak.

Special thanks to Sandra & Ben Doller, 1913 Press and Fanny Howe.

Thank you to Peter Gizzi and Cole Swensen.

Thank you to my teachers at the Iowa Writers' Workshop and Connie Brothers. Also Seth Abramson, Louis Armand, Phil Cairney, Rachel Claiden, Rebecca Dunham, Katie Edwards, Megan Garr and Versal, Dora Malech, Tom McCarthy, Vicki Mahaffey, g. emil reutter.

This book is for my family: Don, Sandra, Neil & Sanna, and Wade—thank you.

MORE TITLES FROM 1913 PRESS:

The Transfer Tree, Karena Youtz (2012)
Conversities, Dan Beachy-Quick & Srikanth Reddy (2012)
Home/Birth: A Poemic, Arielle Greenberg & Rachel Zucker (2011)
Wonderbender, Diane Wald (2011)
Ozalid, Biswamit Dwibedy (2010)
Sightings, Shin Yu Pai (2007)
Seismosis, John Keene & Christopher Stackhouse (2006)
Read, an annual anthology of intertranslation, Sarah Riggs & Cole Swensen, eds.
1913 a journal of forms, Issues 1-6

FORTHCOMING:

Kala Pani, Monica Mody (2013)
Strong Suits, Brad Flis (2013)
The Wrong Book, Nathaniel Otting (2013)
Hg-the liquid, Ward Tietz (2013)
Big House/Disclosure, Mendi & Keith Obadike (2013)
Four Electric Ghosts, Mendi & Keith Obadike (2013)

1913 titles are distributed solely by Small Press Distribution
www.spdbooks.org
& printed on recycled papers.

VALENTINE DE SAINT-POINT

Lust is a force.

FUTURIST MANIFESTO OF LUST, 1913